United States Presidents

Woodrow Wilson

Series Consultant:
Don M. Coerver, professor of history
Texas Christian University, Fort Worth, Texas

Anne Schraff

Enslow Publishers, Inc.

40 Industrial Road	PO Box 38
Box 398	Aldershot
Berkeley Heights, NJ 07922	Hants GU12 6BP
USA	UK

http://www.enslow.com

Library of Congress Cataloging-in-Publication Data

Schraff, Anne E.
   Woodrow Wilson / Anne Schraff
       p. cm. — (United States Presidents)
   Includes bibliographical references and index.
   Summary: Traces the life of the twenty-eighth president, from his
childhood, through his years of extensive writing, to his terms as
president and his involvement in the end of World War I and the
founding of the League of Nations.
   ISBN 0-89490-936-3
   1. Wilson, Woodrow, 1856-1924—Juvenile literature.
   2. Presidents—United States—Biography—Juvenile literature.
   [1. Wilson, Woodrow, 1856-1924. 2. Presidents.] I. Title.
   II. Series.
   E767.S25 1998
   973.91'3'092—dc21
   [B]   97-4372
                                                            CIP
                                                             AC
Printed in the United States of America

10 9 8 7 6 5 4 3

To Our Readers: We have done our best to make sure all Internet
addresses in this book were active and appropriate when we went to press.
However, the author and the publisher have no control over and assume no
liability for the material available on those Internet sites or on other Web
sites they may link to. Any comments or suggestions can be sent by e-mail
to comments@enslow.com or to the address on the back cover.

Illustration Credits: Library of Congress, pp. 11, 26, 32, 37, 38,
43, 45, 55, 57, 84; National Archives, pp. 59, 70, 71, 75, 76, 78, 79,
81, 82.

Source Document Credits: American Political Items Collectors,
pp. 33, 34, 36, 58, 60, 65, 68, 98; Library of Congess, p. 90;
National Archives, pp. 93, 95.

Cover Illustration: White House Historical Association.

Contents

1

ON THE MAYFLOWER

W orld War I had just ended. More soldiers died in that war than in any other in the history of humanity. If all the soldiers killed in the war had marched in formation, twenty abreast, from dawn to sunset every day, it would have taken them four months to pass by a fixed spot.[1] Now, in 1919, President Woodrow Wilson wanted to make sure there would never be another world war.

Wilson was on the most important mission of his life. He wanted the United States to join the League of Nations—an organization designed to settle disputes among nations and keep the peace. But some senators did not want the United States to join. Wilson was taking his cause to the people of the United States. He planned a train trip. He would make speeches all over the Midwest and West.

In September 1919, Wilson was not well. He was thin and tired. He often trembled. His doctor, Cary Grayson, told Wilson not to go on this train trip. Grayson feared the journey might kill Wilson.

Wilson said, "I cannot put my personal safety, my health, in the balance against my duty. I must go."[2] Wilson said he had sent many American soldiers into battle during World War I. He said they had fought and died. "They did not turn back," he said, "and I cannot turn back now."[3]

On the evening of September 2, 1919, Wilson and his wife, Edith, boarded the train—the *Mayflower.* They rolled out of Washington's Union Station. The trip would take twenty-seven days. Wilson would travel ten thousand miles and make thirty major speeches. The *Mayflower* would go all the way to California and back to Washington, D.C.

The first stop was Columbus, Ohio. There, few people came to hear Wilson speak. Later, in Indiana, the crowds were bigger. When the train reached St. Louis, Missouri, the crowds were even larger. Wilson called those who opposed the League of Nations "un-American."[4]

Often children crowded around the train. That touched Wilson's heart. He looked at the children and told them this trip was for them. If there were ever another world war, these children would be the soldiers dying in it.[5]

It was hot when the train reached Kansas City, Kansas. The inside of the *Mayflower* was like an oven.[6] Wilson got hoarse as he shouted his speech. He had no microphone. He stood for hours shaking hands with hundreds of people.

The *Mayflower* traveled about four hundred miles a day. In Des Moines, Iowa, the streets were jammed with people. Wilson stood for a long time waving to them as the train passed. But at night, Wilson was having trouble sleeping. He was getting bad headaches and was constantly tired.

In spite of this, Wilson went on to Nebraska, the Dakotas, Idaho, and then Seattle, Washington. The crowds cheered in a "continuous and riotous uproar."[7] The crowds grew bigger in every city. But Dr. Grayson was worried. Wilson's headaches were so bad that he could not see. Grayson wrote, "the strains" of the last few days were "evident."[8] Clearly, Wilson was not well.

When the train reached Portland, Oregon, Wilson could not sleep at all. He had a bad cough. In Cheyenne, Wyoming, a reporter saw a look of almost "inexpressible weariness" on Wilson's face.[9]

In the Sierra Nevada mountains of California, smoke and heat from the forest fires raging in the area blistered the paint on the *Mayflower*. Wilson had trouble breathing. The left side of his face twitched. But in San Diego he spoke to forty thousand cheering people for more than an hour. He was winning people over. He was convincing them that the United States should join the League of Nations.

By September 22, the *Mayflower* was heading back East. In Salt Lake City, Utah, Wilson was so weak that his wife, Edith, gave him medicine to revive him.[10] As Wilson left the platform, he was soaked in perspiration. Edith Wilson and Dr. Grayson begged him to rest. "No," said Wilson. He felt he was winning the people over and he dared not quit now.[11] Wilson was warned that he might die. "I don't care if I die the next minute after the treaty [League of Nations] is ratified," he said.[12]

On September 25, the *Mayflower* arrived in Pueblo, Colorado. Wilson stumbled onto the speaker's platform. Tears filled his eyes as he begged for support for the League of Nations. Many in the crowd cried too.

Twenty miles from Pueblo, the *Mayflower* stopped. Wilson took a walk to revive himself. At the small town of Rocky Ford, Colorado, five thousand waited to hear Wilson. He was too tired to speak but "he stood there and waved his hand."[13]

Edith Wilson called that evening "the longest and most heartbreaking of my life."[14] At 11:30 P.M. Wilson called out to his wife. She came and sat by his side through the night. Edith Wilson said her husband was "so piteously ill."[15] The next speech was to be in Wichita, Kansas. A large crowd waited.

In the morning Wilson shaved and got dressed. But he was sick to his stomach and was drooling from the left side of his mouth. He wanted to continue the trip. He said he did not want to be a "quitter."[16] But soon even Wilson knew he was terribly sick. "I am going to pieces," he said.[17]

Dr. Grayson cancelled the rest of the trip. With a pilot engine running ahead to clear the tracks, the *Mayflower* raced seventeen hundred miles toward Washington. The speeding train seemed to Edith Wilson "like a funeral cortege [procession]."[18] She looked at her gravely ill husband and she remembered thinking, "I felt that life would never be the same; that something had broken inside me."[19] From then on Edith Wilson would have to hide from the public exactly how sick her husband was. She would even have to hide it from Woodrow Wilson himself.[20]

2

MORAL BEGINNINGS

Thomas Woodrow Wilson was born in Staunton, Virginia, on December 28, 1856. His mother said Tommy was a "fine, healthy fellow."[1] He had two older sisters, Marion and Anne. While Tommy was still a baby the family moved to Augusta, Georgia. Tommy was at the front gate of his house one day in 1860 when he heard someone pass by and say that "Mr. Lincoln was elected and there would be war."[2]

Joseph Ruggles Wilson, Tommy's father, was a teacher and a Presbyterian minister. He was a big, handsome man with bright brown eyes who loved books. He taught Tommy how to read and write. Often father and son would take walks all over the city. Tommy's father would take the boy into mills and warehouses. He explained to Tommy how all the huge machines worked.

Woodrow Wilson later said that his father was "one of the most inspiring fathers that a lad was ever blessed with." Wilson also called his father "the best instructor, the most inspiring companion that a youngster ever had."[3]

Tommy's father played chess and billiards with his son, and once they had a wild game of tag. The game started inside the house and Joseph Wilson scrambled after his son around chairs and tables. Then Tommy ran outside into the garden. His father dodged around trees

The Wilson family home in Staunton, Virginia, is where Thomas Woodrow Wilson was born and lived until age one.

after him. Finally Tommy's father grabbed the boy and shouted, "I've caught him, the young rascal. I've caught him."[4]

Janet "Jessie" Woodrow was a shy young woman with gray eyes and curly brown hair. She and Joseph Wilson were married in 1849. She was called "a typical gentlewoman, delicate, refined, quiet, and dignified in manner." But she had a strong will as well.[5] She enjoyed raising beautiful flowers, and she was a loving mother. Wilson remembered her this way: "I clung to her (a laughed-at mamma's boy) till I was a great big fellow: but love of the best womanhood came to me and entered my heart through those apron-strings."[6]

Tommy always counted on his mother to love him no matter what. Tommy's father was more willing to criticize the boy when he made a mistake.[7]

During the Civil War, Tommy saw much misery. His father's church and yard became a campground and hospital for Confederate soldiers. Young men missing eyes and limbs lay groaning on makeshift beds. All his life he would fear and hate war for causing such suffering.

When Tommy was ten years old, his brother, Joseph Wilson, Jr. was born. Now the Wilsons had four children. The family sang, read, prayed, and played together. Tommy's father would read aloud from serious and funny books. Tommy's mother would sit close by, knitting. The children would be stretched out on the floor. Sometimes Tommy's father joined them. At a funny part of a book he would roar with laughter. Tommy loved to hear his father laugh.[8]

Tommy was slow to learn. He did not read easily until he was eleven years old. He was taught by his father and he did not go to school in his early years. Historians disagree on why it took so long for Tommy to read well. Since his father read aloud from books every night, perhaps the boy saw no urgent need to learn to read himself. Or perhaps he suffered from dyslexia, a reading problem. People with dyslexia reverse the order of the letters of words, reading "was" for "saw," or mixing up *b* and *d* when they appear together in a sentence.

Tommy had a lot of imagination and he enjoyed many adventures during his childhood. He and his friends often dressed up as Native Americans and charged through the woods in mock battles. He said later that "I lived a dream life when I was a lad . . . all the world seemed to me a place of heroic adventures."[9]

Tommy was a wiry little boy who loved baseball. His team was called the Lightfoots and they played for fun on the weekends. Tommy also enjoyed galloping around on his horse.

In 1870, when Tommy was fourteen, the family moved to Columbia, South Carolina. Tommy became interested in ships even though he had never seen the ocean. The only body of water he had seen was the Savannah River. But he filled his sketchbooks with drawings of ships and details about them. He drew marvelous ships with detailed rigging (cables and ropes that support the sails). Tommy knew what each sail did. He understood the roles of skysails and topsails.

In his early teens Tommy felt he was being personally called by God to live a more religious life. Before that he had gone to church because his family did. Now he felt the need for personal prayer, and he read the Bible daily. He said when he became an adult, "My life would not be worth living if it were not for the driving power of religion."[10]

When Tommy was sixteen, reading and taking notes still posed problems. So he taught himself shorthand, a system of writing quickly by substituting symbols for words or phrases. Typewriters were just coming out then too. Tommy used the typewriter to make up for his slow writing.

In Columbia, Tommy attended a private school run by Charles Barnwell. Fifty boys were taught in a barn-like building behind Barnwell's house. They studied Latin and Greek. Each boy's family paid eight dollars a month. Barnwell said of Tommy that he was "extremely dignified," and that "he was not like the other boys. He had a queer way of going off by himself."[11] Yet Tommy always helped the younger students and he was popular with the other boys. He spent about three years in that school.

The Wilsons then moved to Wilmington, North Carolina, right on the Atlantic Ocean. At last Tommy could see the ocean and the ships he loved so much. He often ran down to the harbor to see the ships close up.

He climbed over them, looking at every detail. Once he was seriously injured when he fell from one of the ships.

Tommy Wilson left home for the first time in the autumn of 1873. He was sixteen years old. He attended Davidson College in North Carolina. It was a small Presbyterian college, but Wilson was not happy there. He was homesick. Wilson's mother missed her son too. She wrote him sad letters saying she had headaches all the time from worrying about him. "Do be careful, my dear boy," she wrote.[12] She was afraid her son would not take good care of himself on his own.

Wilson got a bad cold at Davidson and it seemed to get worse and worse. He wrote his mother about how sick he felt and she begged him to come home. He was very happy to do that. He hurried home and spent the next year studying at home. He studied Greek and Latin. He also wrote some articles for a church newspaper, the *North Carolina Presbyterian.* Even at the age of seventeen, Wilson showed that he had a way with words.

At about this time, Wilson dropped the name Tommy and began using Woodrow as his first name. He thought it was a more suitable and dignified name for a young man. He made plans to enter Princeton University. In 1875, eighteen-year-old Woodrow Wilson arrived at Princeton. It was called The College of New Jersey at that time. Wilson had a long face, large ears, gray eyes and sandy blond hair. He was a shy and gangling boy. Wilson's parents thought he might study for the ministry and follow in his father's footsteps. But Wilson did not want to do that. Even though he had been miserable at Davidson College, he loved Princeton. He called his years at Princeton "magical years."[13]

Wilson found many new friends at Princeton. He was a popular freshman. He studied modern history, politics, and literature. He organized the debating club. He became the managing editor of the student newspaper, *The Princetonian*. He also headed the baseball association. Wilson found that he liked politics, so he and several other students made a pact. They promised each other they would use their brains and energy to get power. Then they would use that power to establish the principles they believed in.[14] Wilson was only a teenager, but already he thought about forming high principles and living by them.

Both of Wilson's parents had strong principles. They would discuss every book they read and ask their children to explain the rights and wrongs of actions in the book. As a very young boy, Wilson was inspired especially by *The Life of George Washington* by Mason Weems.[15] Like many writers of that time, Weems used biography to teach moral lessons. For example, he first told the tale of young George Washington chopping down the cherry tree and telling his father the truth about his actions. The cherry tree story is probably not true, but Weems was more interested in moral lessons than facts. The principles that young Wilson had as a boy never changed during his life.

Wilson hoped he would become a political leader or a statesman. He thought a law degree was the road to that end. In 1879, Wilson graduated from Princeton, thirty-eighth in a class of 107 men. Wilson felt very sad at leaving Princeton and his friends. "The parting went harder than I feared even," he wrote to a friend.[16] But in the fall of 1879, Wilson enrolled at the University of Virginia Law School in Charlottesville, Virginia. He felt no liking for the law, but he thought he needed it for his future career as a world leader. "A statesman who is unacquainted with the law is as helpless as the soldier who is ignorant of the use of arms," Wilson said.[17]

Wilson began to study law, but quickly realized he didn't like it at all. Wilson did not even want to open his law books. He liked history books better. So he read them instead of the law books.

Word got back to Wilson's father that the young man was not serious about studying law. Wilson's father wrote to his son urging him to study his law books or face failure.[18]

Wilson decided to drop out of school instead. He left the University of Virginia Law School. He did not get his law degree, but he still had a chance to take a test called the bar exam and become a lawyer. If he got a good grade on the test, he would pass the bar and be able to practice law. Wilson went home and studied his law books there. He found he could study better at home. Then, in May 1882, Wilson passed the bar exam and became a lawyer.

Woodrow Wilson joined another lawyer in Atlanta, Georgia. Together, they started a law practice. But Wilson found out he still did not like the law. He had not liked studying it and now he disliked practicing it. Wilson was twenty-six years old and he hated his job. What was he going to do?

3

WRITER AND EDUCATOR

W oodrow Wilson had a law office, but he spent his time reading and writing articles. He was very interested in government. He admired the British form of government with Parliament and a Prime Minister.

Wilson's father wrote another scolding letter asking his son to take the law more seriously.[1] But Wilson had a new idea. He still wanted a political career, but maybe law was not the road to follow. He thought it might be better to become a teacher. He would teach government and political science, subjects he loved. But that meant going back to school. That fall, in 1883, Wilson decided to enter Johns Hopkins University in Baltimore, Maryland. He wanted to study government and history.

But first he had to make a business trip to Rome,

Georgia. When he went to worship at the local church on Sunday, Wilson saw a very attractive young woman. Later Wilson recalled thinking, "What a bright, pretty face. I'll lay a wager that this demure little lady has lots of life and fun in her."[2]

The young woman was Ellen Louise Axson, the daughter of a minister. Twenty-three years old, Axson had lost her mother three years earlier. She had become like a mother to her younger brother and sister. She was so busy caring for her siblings and her ailing father that she had given up the idea of getting married.[3]

In April 1883, Wilson decided he was in love with Axson. He begged her to take a carriage ride with him. After a picnic, Wilson and Axson went for a nine-mile buggy ride to a small woodsy stream. They talked for a long time. They both loved books, and Axson had begun to like Wilson.

Wilson and Axson wrote letters to each other over the summer, and in September 1883, Wilson proposed marriage. Axson accepted and they were engaged. But they could not get married for some time. Wilson was going to college and Axson wanted to nurse her father back to health.

Ellen Axson was a fine painter and she had hoped for an art career. She knew that if she married Wilson this would not happen. But her mind and her heart told her she should marry Wilson. She wrote, "This is the man I most honor, admire, and look up to, as well as the only one I can love." She decided she would spend her life "with him and for him."[4]

At Johns Hopkins University, Wilson studied history and international law. He joined the literary society and the glee club. He finished his doctoral thesis, *Congressional Government*, and sent it off to a publisher. Six weeks later Wilson got a letter from the publisher, accepting his book. Wilson was overjoyed. Ellen wrote to him, "I don't believe any young man in America ever had such a brilliant triumph."[5]

Wilson's book was published in 1885. In it he said that congressional committees had too much power. He explained that a new law was often blocked in committee. In that case Congress never even gets the chance to see it, and then the people never even know who blocked the bill. The committee just buries it under a ton of paper. Wilson said that when a law is not passed the people should know who to blame. "How is the schoolmaster, the nation, to know which boy needs the whipping?" Wilson asked.[6] He wanted the people to know which congressperson should be blamed.

Wilson also criticized the power of lobbies. Lobbies are groups of people who put pressure on Congress for their own special interests. Sometimes lobbies influence members of Congress to vote in favor of a law the lobby wants. The wishes of the people do not count as much with the congressperson. Wilson was upset that by winning over one powerful congressperson, the lobby could kill a bill many people favored. Wilson complained that clever lobbyists "gained the ear of the House itself."[7]

Wilson's book made many good points. Those who read the book were impressed with the young author's mind. Though just twenty-nine years old, Wilson had pointed to real flaws in Congress.

On June 24, 1885, Woodrow Wilson and Ellen Axson were married in her father's church in Savannah, Georgia. The young couple spent the rest of the summer in a cottage in the nearby hills. It was a very happy time for them. Wilson was not yet working, but he had finished college.

In 1886 Wilson received a doctoral degree in history and political science from Johns Hopkins University. He got his first teaching job at Bryn Mawr, an all-women's college outside Philadelphia.

Bryn Mawr had forty-two students and seven professors. The library shelves had very few books. The Wilsons, along with the other faculty, lived together in a house on campus. The Wilsons had two upstairs rooms to themselves, but all the faculty ate together in a large dining room. Wilson taught ancient Greek and Roman history, but he did not enjoy it much. At that time most men looked at women's education as less important than men's education. Wilson felt that way too. He was worried that teaching women would cause his mind to grow lazy. "I have for a long time been hungry for a class of men," he said.[8]

In April 1886 the Wilsons' first child, Margaret, was

born. In August 1887 their second daughter, Jessie, was born. Wilson was working on another book, *The State,* and actively seeking another job.

In 1888 Wilson got his wish. Wesleyan University in Middletown, Connecticut, hired him. In 1889 *The State* was published and the third Wilson child, Eleanor, was born. The Wilsons and their three daughters settled in at Wesleyan. Wilson organized a student debating society. He helped coach the winning football team. He also began work on a long history book.

In 1890 a call came from Princeton University—the college where Wilson had been so happy as a student. Now they wanted him to teach law at Princeton. Wilson accepted the offer. When the word spread that Woodrow Wilson was teaching a course, half the school signed up. The students knew of his books and his fine teaching reputation at Wesleyan. Wilson was brimming with excitement at the idea of teaching at Princeton. He said that at Princeton he felt "like a man feeling the bit of a spirited horse capable of any speed and with wind for any race."[9]

The students liked Wilson right away. One of his students, Frederick Jackson Turner, later became a famous historian. Turner remembered Wilson as "homely, solemn, young, glum, but with that fire in his face and eye that means that its possessor is not of the common crowd."[10] Though stern in the classroom, Wilson sat up late at night talking as friends with his students. He often shared jokes with them in this informal setting.

Ellen Wilson was happy at Princeton too. She enjoyed concerts, plays, and friendship with the other families.[11] The Wilson daughters tumbled happily on the lovely campus greens.

The Wilsons spent twelve years at Princeton. Wilson became the leader of a group of professors who wanted to make big changes at the college. Wilson wanted the students and teachers to have a close relationship. He wanted small classes so all the students had the chance to ask questions and discuss ideas. Thousands of Wilson's students at Princeton said he was the greatest teacher they ever had. Year after year he was voted the most popular teacher at Princeton.[12]

Wilson was also asked to travel around the United States to give lectures. He wrote many magazine articles. In 1897 his biography of George Washington was published. In 1902 his five-volume *History of the American People* was published. Wilson wrote in a dramatic, flowery style. Here is a sample of how he described the Salem witch trials:

> In 1692 a distemper showed itself at Salem in Massachusetts, which seemed for a little blacker than war itself—an ominous distemper of the mind. It was the year of the frenzy against what men fancied to be witchcraft, and Salem, where the chief madness was, saw nineteen persons swing upon her gallows hill for commerce with the devil.[13]

When he was not teaching or writing, Wilson enjoyed being with his family. He wanted his children to enjoy the same kind of warm family life he had loved as a boy. So Wilson would gather his daughters together and tell them funny stories. Wilson read poetry and other books to them as his own father had done with his children. Wilson loved to change his voice and mimic people to make his daughters laugh. There were many jolly family singalongs around the piano. Daughter Margaret's interest in a singing career was nurtured there. Woodrow Wilson was happiest when he was relaxing with his family.

On June 9, 1902, Wilson became president of Princeton University. He was forty-six years old. He now had the chance to make all the improvements he dreamed of. He ordered new buildings where classes could be held.

Wilson also set up the preceptorial system. In the past, most classes at Princeton were taught in this way—many students sat in a large lecture hall. The professor lectured and the students took notes. Because there were so many students there was little time for discussion. Wilson wanted to change all of this. He wanted many young professors—called preceptors—to be hired. They would hold small classes where students could talk as much as the teacher. Wilson believed this made for a better education.

Wilson described the kind of student he wanted Princeton to turn out: "cultured and well-rounded."[14] Wilson also wanted only the very best students to enroll at Princeton.

Once a young man failed the entrance examination

Woodrow Wilson became president of Princeton University in 1902.

to Princeton. The young man's father came to see Wilson. He begged Wilson to let his son come to Princeton, even though the young man was not very bright. Wilson said, "If the angel Gabriel applied for admission to Princeton University and could not pass the entrance examination, he would not be admitted."[15]

Another time the mother of a student was upset when her son was expelled from Princeton for cheating. She pleaded with Wilson to let her son back in. She told Wilson she would die if her son did not get back into Princeton. Wilson answered her, "If I had to choose between your life, or my life, or anybody's life and the good of this college, I should choose the good of the college."[16] The young man was not allowed back into Princeton. When Wilson believed he was right, he would not budge. That was the kind of man he was throughout his life.

Wilson worked very hard at Princeton. He drove himself to do more work every day. In May 1906, he awoke one morning blind in his left eye. He probably had suffered a stroke. A stroke happens when blood going to the brain is blocked. After a stroke a person may be paralyzed, or lose sight or speech. Wilson was just forty-nine years old. The doctors ordered him to rest. Wilson and his family took a long vacation to England and Scotland. His left eye regained most of its sight and he felt better. Wilson returned to Princeton to continue his plans to improve the college.

At Princeton there were student clubs where

wealthy young men lived and ate. Wilson thought this system was bad. He wanted all Princeton students to mix together. He wanted all social and academic activities to include students of all social classes.

Wilson's idea for more mixed socializing started a big fight. The student eating clubs were an old tradition. The professors and students who liked them wanted to keep them. Wilson was saddened by the bitter opposition to his ideas.[17]

On June 26, 1910, Wilson was invited to meet with a group of businessmen and politicians. They had been watching Wilson for a long time and had read his books. They told Wilson he was just the man they were looking for. They wanted him to run for governor of New Jersey.

Wilson promised to think very hard about the offer. Years before, as a student, Wilson had dreamed of a political career. Wilson loved teaching at Princeton, but the recent fighting over the eating clubs would make it easier to leave. Now seemed like the perfect time to reach for his youthful dream of a political career.

In October 1910, Wilson resigned as president of Princeton to prepare for a brand new career.

4

THE "NEW FREEDOM"

The Democrat who led the party in 1910 was William Jennings Bryan. He made many speeches against wealthy businessmen. He wanted to help small farmers and workers. Some men in the Democratic party were afraid of Bryan. They wanted a candidate who was for big business. Many thought Woodrow Wilson was that man. They wanted to help him become governor of New Jersey. They hoped this would be a stepping stone to the presidency of the United States.

Wilson did seem to be against the ideas of Bryan. Wilson agreed with conservative Democrats in 1906 that Bryan should be tossed "into a cocked hat"[1] (removed from political life). But when Wilson was elected governor of New Jersey in 1910, his supporters had a surprise coming. Wilson began supporting progressive measures. He wanted senators to be elected by the people, not by state legislatures. He wanted primary elections so people could choose presidential candidates. He also enforced controls on what railroads charged to ship goods.

When Wilson became governor in 1911, he promised to serve the people with a "singleness of purpose."[2] The first thing he did was to take control of the Democratic party away from the bosses. These were powerful men who tried to block laws they did not like. Wilson said he would defend the interests of the ordinary people against the bosses.[3]

Wilson had many fights with the powerful political bosses.[4] The bosses favored laws protecting the rights of big business. They opposed laws, for example, that permitted trade unions.

Wilson enjoyed being governor of New Jersey. He even enjoyed the ceremonial duties like presiding over state dinners and reviewing the National Guard, dressed in tail coat and top hat, riding a horse past the troops.

As governor, Wilson formed a public service commission. It controlled railroad and public utilities prices. Wilson also started an insurance system for disabled workers. If injured on the job, workers would still be able to receive an income.

Wilson was governor for only a few months when the Wilson-for-president movement started. The first group started in Staunton, Virginia. Soon, others formed. Wilson was not yet sure he even wanted to be president. But he did agree to undertake a speaking tour to find out how people would react to him when he spoke about his ideas.

Wilson made speeches in the western United States. He spoke about the "common man" who was unfairly treated by selfish business interests.[5] In Denver, Colorado, Wilson was surprised to find twelve thousand people waiting to hear him speak. He said the "finger of God" is against those who would harm the people.[6] Wilson was deeply moved by how much the people seemed to like him. "It daunts me to see their admiration and trust," he said.[7]

In 1908 Wilson wrote that an effective president can do a great deal of good if he has "character, modesty, devotion and insight as well as force."[8] After his trip, Wilson felt sure he could be a good president. He decided to run for president of the United States.

At the Democratic Convention in June 1912, there were many men battling for the nomination. Leading the pack was Speaker of the House Champ Clark from Missouri who was favored by some progressives, and conservative Congressman Oscar Underwood of Alabama. Would the party choose an old party regular like Clark or Underwood or choose somebody like Wilson who was not entangled in the old ways? Clark won more votes than the other candidates on the first nine ballots, but he couldn't get a majority. On the thirtieth ballot, Wilson was leading. On the forty-sixth ballot, he was finally chosen as the Democratic candidate for president.

William Howard Taft was chosen by the Republicans to run for reelection in 1912. Former President Theodore Roosevelt started his own party—the Progressive or Bull Moose Party. It was a three-way race. The people who usually voted Republican now divided their votes between Taft and Roosevelt.

Theodore Roosevelt and William Howard Taft disliked each other. But Roosevelt liked Wilson. He

Here, Woodrow Wilson campaigns for the presidency in 1912.

SOURCE DOCUMENT

A 1912 campaign poster features Wilson and running mate Thomas Marshall.

called Wilson an able man who would make an excellent president.[9]

Taft did not enjoy being president. He did not campaign for reelection at all. He just made a few written speeches giving his opinion on the issues. So the election was really just between Roosevelt and Wilson.

Roosevelt was afraid that the government was getting too big and powerful. He attacked the Democrats and Republicans as servants of the "rich few."[10] But in truth both Wilson and Roosevelt wanted the government to regulate business when its practices were harmful to the people. Wilson, however, also

A 1912 Wilson campaign poster

feared big government. "The history of liberty is the history of the limitation of government power," Wilson said.[11]

Theodore Roosevelt's plan was called "New Nationalism" while Wilson's program was called "New Freedom." Both favored social welfare laws, permitting women to vote, and improving the rights of labor. The only real difference was which man could best carry out these progressive ideas.

In the 1912 election, Taft came in third, winning only Vermont and Utah. Roosevelt won six states and came in second. Woodrow Wilson was elected president with 42 percent of the vote. That means more Americans voted against him than for him, but Wilson got more votes than anybody else. If the Republican vote had not been divided, the outcome of the election might well have been different.

On November 16, the Wilsons sailed to Bermuda for a vacation. It was a wonderful time for the family before Wilson took on the office of president. Wilson slept late, chatted with the other ship passengers, and had a good time. In Bermuda the Wilsons lived in a seaside cottage. They took carriage and bicycle rides. In December 1912, Wilson had to resign as governor of New Jersey. Then he went to Washington to choose his cabinet.

Thomas R. Marshall was Wilson's vice-president. William Jennings Bryan would serve as secretary of state and Wilson's campaign manager, William G. McAdoo, became secretary of the treasury.

SOURCE DOCUMENT

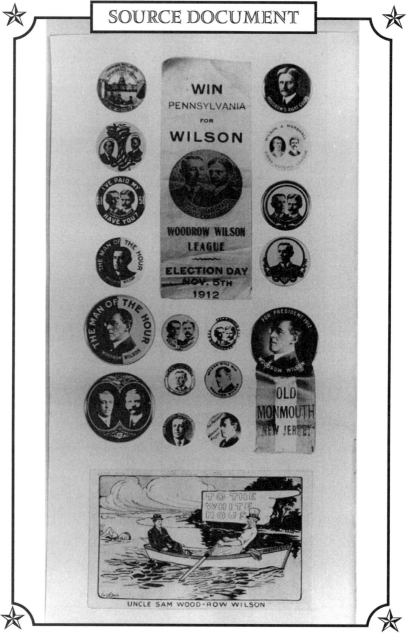

Buttons and memorabilia from the 1912 election accompany a campaign political cartoon.

Wilson chose Edward M. House to be his personal advisor. House was a rich Texan who was nicknamed Colonel House. Wilson called House his second personality. "His thoughts and mine are one," Wilson once said.[12] House would remain with Wilson throughout his entire presidency.

On Inauguration Day, President Taft was very happy. "Mr. President," he said to Wilson, "I hope you'll be happy here. I'm glad to be going. This is the loneliest place in the world."[13]

Wilson's inauguration speech showed how seriously

Wilson (middle) on his way to inauguration with outgoing President William Howard Taft (left). Taft was glad to be out of the presidency.

he took his new job. He said that people everywhere had high hopes that he would do a good job. He hoped he would not disappoint them. He promised to try hard.[14]

That night fireworks lit up the sky in Washington, D.C. Ellen Wilson did not want to have the usual inauguration ball, so the Wilson family and their relatives gathered in the White House for a small party.

Wilson was fifty-six years old when he became president. He was trim, agile, and his hair was streaked with

Wilson and his family on the White House lawn, shortly after his victory over William Howard Taft in 1912. From left to right: Margaret, Ellen Axson Wilson, Eleanor, Jessie, and Woodrow Wilson.

gray. He had many colds and often he had stomach trouble. The sight in his left eye never completely returned. The White House doctor, Cary T. Grayson, worried from the beginning that Wilson was not in good health. The stroke Wilson had suffered in 1906 was a bad sign. It meant Wilson's arteries, which carried blood to his brain, were partly blocked. He was in danger of having another stroke.

Dr. Grayson devoted the rest of his life to helping Wilson stay as healthy as he could so he could do his job as president. But Dr. Grayson wanted Wilson to get plenty of rest. Wilson, however, was used to working hard. He wanted to do so many things. He hoped to make America, and the rest of the world, a better place. So Dr. Grayson did not succeed in slowing Wilson down. Wilson bounded into his job as president like a racehorse leaving the gate.

5

THE GREAT
WAR ERUPTS

N ot since the administration of John Adams had a United States president addressed both houses of Congress in person. On April 7, 1913, Woodrow Wilson stood before the members of Congress to tell them what his program would be. Wilson did this so the members of Congress could see that the president "is a person, not a mere department of the government."[1]

Wilson wanted the tariffs to be cut. Tariffs are taxes placed on items bought from a foreign country. The Underwood Tariff was passed in October 1913. It lowered the tax on 958 imported items. Tariffs were now lower than they had been in fifty years. It was a step toward free world trade. Another part of this bill established an income tax on all incomes over $3,000 a year.

Wilson was very pleased with the lower tariff. When he signed the bill into law he said, "I feel tonight like a man who is lodging happily in the inn which lies halfway along the journey. We have served our fellow men and have thereby tried to serve God."[2]

Also during Wilson's first year, the Federal Reserve Act was passed. It created twelve districts in the United States, each with a federal reserve bank. The government chose experts to set national interest rates. Interest rates are charged for people taking loans to buy houses, cars and other things. When interest rates are low, people can afford to buy more. Then the economy improves. When interest rates are high, people buy less. Sometimes this causes a recession. The twelve Federal Reserve banks issued money and worked with local banks. The Federal Reserve Act was called the most important success Wilson had had.

The Wilsons settled into the White House with their daughters, Eleanor and Jessie. Daughter Margaret lived in New York and trained for a singing career. Ellen Wilson was a quiet first lady. She entertained only when she had to. She fixed up the White House garden. She always tried hard to make life homey and comfortable for her husband.

Ellen Wilson was deeply interested in social work. There were thousands of mostly African-American families living under poor conditions only a few blocks from the White House. Their houses lacked running water and bathrooms, and ill-fitting doors and windows let insects in. Ellen Wilson took members of Congress down to see these slums. She kept on doing this until a slum clearance bill was introduced in Congress. This bill would provide money to build better housing to replace the broken-down buildings where people now lived.

In her spare time, Ellen Wilson also returned to her old love of painting. She painted fine landscapes. She did some of her best work while she lived at the White House.

Wilson enjoyed life at the White House with his family. On doctor's orders he spent part of each day playing golf. But nothing relaxed him so much as being with his family. He especially enjoyed his daughter Eleanor, because she laughed at his jokes and mimicry. He liked to have serious discussions with his daughter Jessie.[3] For a little while it was a happy family group. Then, in November 1913, the family was broken up.

Jessie Wilson married Francis Bowes Sayre. After the White House wedding Wilson admitted that he was very sad to lose a daughter. In spite of his feelings, he pretended to enjoy the wedding. "I feel bereaved," Wilson said. "I know from my own feelings how [Ellen] is suffering and that adds to my own misery."[4] Then, in 1914 twenty-five-year-old Eleanor Wilson married fifty-one-year-old William McAdoo, the secretary of the treasury. Wilson did not like McAdoo to begin with, calling him a boring loudmouth.[5] Now Wilson was crushed to see his last daughter leaving. "She was simply part of me, the only delightful part," Wilson said.[6]

Although he didn't approve of his daughter Eleanor's marriage to Secretary of the Treasury William McAdoo, Wilson adored his granddaughter Ellen Wilson McAdoo.

Wilson had always depended on his warm family circle as a place of refuge from the pressures of his work. Family was very important to him. And just as Wilson was missing his newly married daughters, the worst personal tragedy of his life was beginning.

Ellen Wilson complained of being tired all the time. At first she was sure it was only depression from missing her daughters. Then Dr. Grayson found she was suffering from Bright's Disease—a kidney problem. She also had tuberculosis of the kidneys. Dr. Grayson knew there was nothing that could be done to save Ellen Wilson. But he did not tell the Wilsons. Dr. Grayson feared that such a shock would cause the president to have another stroke.

Ellen Wilson was spending most of her time in bed. Wilson spent long days and nights at her bedside. He wrote his speeches and replied to mail while she slept. He was still "hoping and believing" that she would get well.[7] Even though Ellen Wilson was obviously getting sicker, Wilson refused to accept the terrible truth.

On August 4, 1914, Dr. Grayson told Wilson to call his daughters to the White House. He finally told Wilson that the end was near for Ellen. On August 6, Ellen Wilson made it clear her last wish was passage of the slum clearance bill by Congress. Word was brought to her that this was done. Ellen Wilson had already said her good-byes to her family. Then she smiled and, with her husband holding her hand, she died. The President got up and walked to the window. "Oh my God," he said, "what am I going to do?"[8] Wilson sat beside his wife's dead body for two days and nights. Ellen Wilson's body was then taken to her hometown of Rome, Georgia, for burial.

As the funeral procession reached Myrtle Hill Cemetery, heavy rain came down. Wilson shook with sobs. For a few minutes he stood silently at the grave, then he walked away.

Wilson grieved so much during the days and weeks that followed that he seemed to lose the will to live. He found relief only in working harder than ever. "The day's work must be done," he wrote, "and he [Wilson] must play his full part in doing it. It matters little how much life is left in him when the day is over."[9]

On a walk with his friend and advisor, Colonel

The Wilsons sit inside the White House in 1914, shortly before Ellen Axson Wilson died. Left to right: Margaret, Woodrow, Eleanor, Jessie, and Ellen Axson Wilson

House, in the winter of 1914, Wilson said he did not wish to live anymore. His grief over losing his wife was so great that he could not even do his work.[10] Wilson had written a letter to a friend calling himself "dead in heart and body, weighed down with a leaden indifference and despair."[11]

Wilson's cousin, Helen Bones, said of him at this time, "No one can offer Cousin Woodrow any word of comfort for there is no comfort."[12] Wilson himself said, "Even books have grown meaningless to me. I read detective stories to forget, as a man would get drunk."[13]

During Ellen Wilson's illness and her husband's intense grieving after her death, a mass of foreign policy problems descended on President Wilson. One of the problems concerned Mexico.

Wilson had very strong ideas about Latin America and Mexico. He hoped to promote the cause of democracy there. Many Latin American countries were run by dictators. The people who lived there had little say in their own lives. Wilson hoped that would change. He wanted the United States to push things in the right direction to give democracy a boost.

In 1914 Mexico was in the middle of a civil war. In May 1911, Mexican President Porfirio Diaz, a dictator for over thirty years, had been overthrown. The new Mexican president was Francisco Madero. Madero promised land for the poor and more democracy for the people. Wilson liked Madero. Wilson was glad that Mexico would at last have a democratic government.

However, in February 1913, Madero was overthrown and murdered. The new president was a brutal man named Victoriano Huerta, nicknamed "Mexico's Nero."[14] (Nero was a murderous Roman emperor who killed many innocent people.) President Wilson was furious. He called Huerta "a diverting brute, so false, so sly."[15] Wilson wanted Huerta to resign, but Huerta taunted Wilson. He said he would not get out until both he and Wilson were in hell.[16]

In April 1914, Huerta arrested the crew of an American ship at Tampico, Mexico. This gave Wilson his chance to interfere in Mexico. Wilson ordered the United States Navy to occupy Vera Cruz. He also sent United States Marines. Wilson hoped the American military forces could force Huerta out and bring a better leader to power in Mexico.

In August 1914, Venustiano Carranza overthrew Huerta. Wilson was pleased, but troubles with Mexico continued for a long time. In 1916 a Mexican revolutionary, General Francisco "Pancho" Villa, fought the government of Carranza. Villa and his army, called Villistas, made many armed raids into the United States. Finally, on March 9, 1916, Villa led his men into the United States, attacking the small town of Columbus, New Mexico, and killing nineteen Americans. Wilson ordered Brigadier General John J. "Black Jack" Pershing to cross into Mexico and capture Villa. Pershing led about seven thousand Americans three hundred fifty miles into Mexico, but they never found Villa. Gradually the violence on the United States-Mexico border ceased.

A far greater foreign policy crisis was occurring in Europe during this time. On June 28, 1914, the Austrian Archduke Franz Ferdinand was assassinated. He was the man who was to become leader of Austria-Hungary. The man who killed him was a Serbian. Austria-Hungary wanted to take revenge against Serbia.

Most large European countries were allies of either Austria-Hungary or Serbia. Russia was an ally of Serbia. Germany was allied with Austria-Hungary. England and France sided with Russia. The armies of Europe were getting ready to march against each other. The first shots of World War I were about to be fired. It would become the most murderous war in human history up until that time.

Germany declared war on Russia in August 1914. Two days later, Germany declared war on France. On August 20 the German army entered Brussels, Belgium. For seven hours the gray-uniformed German army marched through Belgium, looking like a river of steel. Britain declared war on Germany.

Like most Americans, Wilson was more sympathetic to the Allies—Britain, France, Russia, and Belgium. Wilson disliked the militarism of Germany. But also like most Americans, Wilson did not want the United States to get into the war. In August 1914, Wilson said the United States must be "impartial in thought as well as action."[17]

At first Wilson did not allow American bankers to loan money to the Allies. He feared that if America loaned money to the Allies, then we would have a stake in the war. Wilson did not want anything to push America closer to war. But then he changed his mind. He permitted rich Americans to loan money to the Allies. The American bankers gave $2 billion to the Allies. The United States was not totally neutral anymore.

Before the start of 1915, Austria-Hungary had invaded Russia. German and French armies were locked in a huge battle on the Marne River in France. Brutal trench warfare was under way. Each side dug trenches about six to eight feet deep and only wide enough for two men to pass. The land between the trenches was called "no man's land." Many men were shot and killed while running between trenches. Often they would lie unburied for days. Their comrades were afraid to recover the bodies lest they too be killed by sniper fire. This trench warfare went on, month after month, year after year.

Woodrow Wilson would have preferred to handle only domestic affairs (those within the United States). However, he was expected to deal with foreign issues as well. He once said that the worst thing that could happen to his presidency would be foreign problems taking up all his time.[18] That is exactly what was happening. But still Wilson tried to carry out his domestic agenda by introducing laws to improve life in the United States.

6

"HE KEPT US OUT OF WAR"

In September 1914, the Federal Trade Commission Act was passed. In passing this, Woodrow Wilson kept his promise to shield small businesses from unfair practices by large companies. For example, three large lumber companies would get together to charge a very low price for a piece of wood. A smaller lumber company would be undercut because it could not sell lumber that cheaply. Then, as soon as the small company was forced out of business, the large companies would all agree to raise prices. The Federal Trade Commission Act made such practices illegal.

In October 1914, the Clayton Act was passed. It protected people who formed unions from being prosecuted as illegal groups. In the past, workers forming unions had sometimes been jailed.

Meanwhile a steady stream of bad news was coming from the war front. Allied ships had blockaded Germany so supplies could not get through. Germany struck back. It threatened to use its submarines to sink any ships carrying supplies to the Allies.

International law was not very clear on this issue. During a war, neutral ships were supposed to be safe from attack. If either of the warring sides halted a merchant ship or a passenger ship, it had the duty to provide for the safety of innocent people aboard. But submarine warfare brought in a new problem. A regular warship could stop another ship and check for arms to make sure it was neutral. Then, if the ship carried weapons, innocent people could be removed before the ship was destroyed. But the frail submarine could not risk being destroyed by deck guns on a ship it stopped. So submarines struck and sunk ships without making provisions for innocent people.

Britain often stopped American ships and took off any goods they believed were being carried to Germany. But this British action did not risk lives. When Germany threatened to sink passenger and merchant ships, lives were in danger. Wilson said "the loss of life is irreparable."[1] He warned the Germans not to harm innocent passengers on oceangoing ships.

In March 1915, the Germans sank the British liner, *Falaba*, and one American passenger died. Some newspapers in the United States wrote angry editorials. Wilson sent a stern note of protest to Germany. But

Secretary of State William Jennings Bryan took a different view. He pointed out that Americans travelling on British ships in a war zone were asking for trouble.

During this difficult period there was an important change in Woodrow Wilson's personal life. About eight months after Ellen Wilson had died, the president was playing golf with Dr. Grayson. It was a cold, rainy day in the spring of 1915. The pair ran into Wilson's cousin and a friend of hers, Edith Bolling Galt. The two women were cleaning mud off their shoes when Wilson asked Grayson, "Who is that beautiful lady?"[2]

Galt was a tall, forty-two-year-old widow with gray eyes and dark hair. Her husband had owned a fine silver and jewelry store. When he died, Galt took over and ran the business successfully. Because she had attracted Wilson's interest, she was invited to the White House. She came for dinner and Wilson found that he enjoyed her company very much. He made plans to see her again soon.

In the weeks that followed, Galt and Wilson took many automobile rides together. By the end of April, Galt was at the White House for dinner every night. On May 3, Wilson was having dinner with Galt when he told her that he loved her. "Oh, you can't love me," Galt said, "for you don't really know me."[3] Wilson continued his courtship of Galt.

On May 7, 1915, Wilson was about to play golf when shocking news reached him. A German submarine had sent a torpedo into a British ship, the

Lusitania. On May 1, 1915, the *Lusitania* had left New York for Liverpool, England. At that time it was the biggest, fastest ship in the world. There were almost two thousand men, women and children on board, including 128 Americans. Prior to its sailing, the German government had posted a notice in New York newspapers warning that any ship bound for England might be sunk. The ship sailed anyway.

The *Lusitania* was ten miles off Ireland when it was hit. In ten minutes the big ship sank. The passengers scrambled desperately to get into lifeboats. Everything happened too fast. Of the 1,198 people who died in the sea, many were children and babies, and 124 were Americans. Wilson listened to the tragic details and paced alone in the rain in front of the White House.

The American people were horrified by the sinking of the *Lusitania*. *The Des Moines Register and Leader* wrote, "the sinking of the *Lusitania* was deliberate murder."[4] In the decades since World War I, tens of thousands of innocent civilians have died in war. Mass bombings of cities have taken millions of lives. But in 1915 the mass death of civilians was a new and brutal development in war. There were angry demands to punish Germany for this outrage. Wilson urged everybody to stay calm. "There is such a thing as a man being too proud to fight," Wilson said.[5] Wilson sent another strong protest to Germany. Once more, Secretary of State Bryan reminded everyone that Americans should not be travelling in the war zone. Bryan was so upset at the idea that the United States might go to war over those incidents that he resigned. The new secretary of state, Robert Lansing, got a promise from Germany to stop submarine attacks on unarmed passenger ships.

Some Americans felt Wilson was not taking strong enough action against Germany. Former President Theodore Roosevelt said Wilson was "stupid and timid."[6] Roosevelt said England and France stood for "humanity and civilization" while Germany stood for the forces of evil.[7]

During the summer of 1915, Wilson wrote many letters to Edith Galt. She wrote warm letters back. Wilson put in a special telephone line between his bedroom and her home so they could talk to each other often. Wilson sent her orchids, her favorite flower, daily. They took rides in his Pierce-Arrow car. Wilson was so joyous one night that he danced up and down the curbs as he walked. He did a little jig as he whistled the popular tune "Oh, You Beautiful Doll."[8]

On December 18, 1915, Wilson married Galt at the White House. It was a small family wedding. The Wilsons sneaked off for a honeymoon in Hot Springs, Arkansas. They tricked the news reporters into thinking they were going somewhere else so they would have some privacy.

In March 1916, an unarmed French ship, the *Sussex* was torpedoed by Germany. Several Americans on the *Sussex* were injured. Wilson warned Germany that the United States would break off diplomatic relations unless submarine attacks on passenger ships ceased at once.[9] In May 1916, Germany said no more merchant ships would be sunk without warning.

That same year, Wilson kept more promises in the area of social welfare. In 1916 the Keating-Owen Act forbade shipments across state lines of products made by child labor. Millions of children between the ages of ten and fifteen worked long hours, often in harsh conditions, in the fields or garment factories. Wilson hoped to reduce this number. The 1916 Adamson Act provided an eight-hour-day for railroad workers. Also in 1916 Wilson appointed Louis D. Brandeis to the Supreme Court. As a lawyer Brandeis had fought for the rights of workers and women seeking justice in the workplace. But many powerful people opposed

Wilson and Edith Bolling Galt, whom he courted and married while running the country.

Brandeis. Six former presidents of the American Bar Association, including ex-President Taft said Brandeis was unfit to be a Supreme Court justice. They believed he did not uphold the strict rules of the United States Constitution and bent them for social welfare causes. Leading businesspeople also opposed Brandeis. Brandeis earned their wrath by speaking out on behalf of ordinary citizens.[10] Wilson supported Brandeis in spite of the opposing voices.[11]

However, it was the war, not the domestic squabbles, that occupied most of Woodrow Wilson's time and energy. During the summer of 1916 thousands of soldiers on both sides were falling in battle. The Battle of Verdun in the French city of Verdun cost about six hundred thousand dead and wounded men. In the Battle of the Somme, also in France, Allied forces pushed the Germans back seven miles. To do that they lost about six hundred thousand to the ranks of the wounded and the dead. The Germans lost the same number of men. World War I had become an awful killing ground. Nobody was winning. Nobody was losing. The battle lines went back and forth. It was called a stalemate.

The American people heard about the tragic slaughter. They did not want American soldiers to get involved. The presidential campaign of 1916 was getting under way. President Wilson ran for reelection against the Republican candidate, Judge Charles Evans Hughes. Hughes spoke out in favor of keeping America

President Wilson in 1916, a year in which he had to deal with German acts of war, as well as the campaign for the second term of his presidency.

SOURCE DOCUMENT

Memorabilia from the 1912 and 1916 election campaigns

neutral. He criticized Wilson on small issues. He did not want to sound aggressive and scare the voters into thinking that he might lead America into war. Wilson was described by his supporters as the president who had kept us out of war. During the final days of the campaign, the chant at every Wilson rally was the same. "He kept us out of war," supporters cried. That was a powerful message. It appealed to most Americans.

When the votes were counted on election day 1916, Woodrow Wilson was reelected narrowly. Wilson won 49 percent of the vote, and Hughes won 46 percent.

As World War I raged on, tales of horror on the battlefield filled newspapers. Men living in trenches stood in putrid water with rats gnawing at their feet. Some of

Wilson's inauguration in 1917 after winning a second term

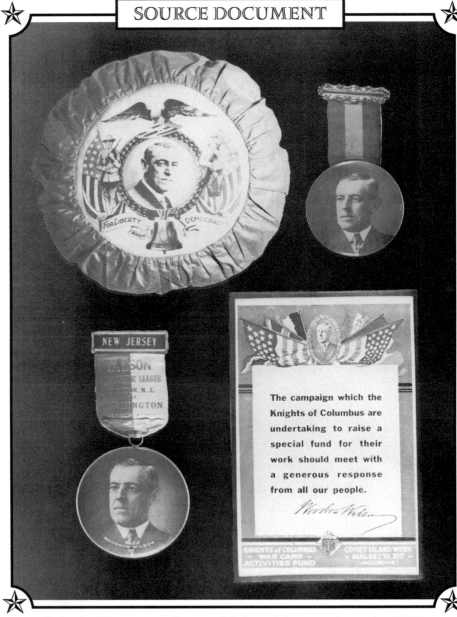

A fundraising poster (lower right) and buttons from the 1916 campaign

the soldiers on duty had come to believe that this was the battle of Armageddon—or the end of the world. Americans wanted no part of it.

Wilson had won reelection by keeping us out of war. Now he faced the daunting task of fulfilling the promise of that campaign chant. Could he continue to keep the United States out of war?

7

SOLDIERS
OF FREEDOM

President Wilson believed the best way to keep the United States out of World War I was to end the war. He worked hard on a peace plan. He wanted to help start real peace talks between the Allies and the Central Powers, led by Germany.

In January 1917, Wilson spoke about his plan for peace. He asked for "peace without victory" where all the nations would be treated fairly.[1] He said that in modern war there are no winners, only losers. So his peace plan would not permit revenge against anybody.[2]

On February 1, Germany announced a policy of unrestricted submarine warfare. This would include attacks on passenger ships. Wilson broke off diplomatic relations with Germany. Then came the Zimmermann telegram. The German foreign secretary sent a coded message to Mexico. He told Mexico that if the United States declared war on Germany, Mexico should attack the United States. Then Germany would help Mexico regain territory it had lost to the United States after the Mexican War. This alarmed the United States. It was another reason to go to war against Germany.

In March 1917, Wilson was sworn into his second term as president. He feared he could not keep his promise to keep the United States out of war. Several more American ships had been sunk.

Wilson was afraid that if the United States did enter the war, the democratic spirit of the country would suffer. "Once lead this people into war," he said, "and they'll forget there ever was such a thing as tolerance. To fight you must be brutal and ruthless, and the spirit of ruthless brutality will enter into the very fibre of our national life, infecting Congress, the courts, the policeman on the beat, the man in the street."[3]

Wilson also believed that the stress of being a wartime president would kill him.[4]

On April 1, 1917, Wilson sat up all night until four in the morning working on a message to Congress. Then he entered the House of Representatives to the great applause of all. The Supreme Court justices and the senators clapped. Visitors cheered. Wilson told this special session that the United States should enter World War I. He said, "the world must be made safe for democracy,"[5] and the actions of Germany amounted to "war against the government and people of the United States."[6]

Wilson spoke for thirty-six minutes. A great tide of cheering exploded when he finished. People shouted and waved little American flags. Wilson walked quickly from the podium. Outside, people on the street cheered as Wilson went by with his secretary, Joseph Tumulty. Later, Wilson turned to Tumulty and said, "my message today was a message of death for our young men. How strange it seems to applaud that." Then, according to Tumulty, Wilson broke down and wept.[7]

The United States Senate approved entering the war on April 4, and the House approved it on April 6.

The United States Navy was ready for immediate action, but the Army had only about one hundred twenty-six thousand men. So in May 1917, a selective service bill was rushed through Congress. All men between the ages of twenty-one and thirty would be eligible to be drafted into the military. General Pershing was put in charge of American forces—called the American Expeditionary Force (AEF). They would go to Europe and fight side-by-side with the English and the French. By the end of World War I the United States had almost 5 million men and women under arms. About 2.75 million were drafted. About one hundred seventeen thousand Americans died in World War I.

Wilson made a stirring speech to American soldiers bound for Europe. He called them the "soldiers of freedom."[8] In June 1917, the first Americans left for the battlefields of France. Hometown crowds sent them off with bands and parades.

SOURCE DOCUMENT

This World War I memorabilia depicts wartime propaganda.

In order to get all Americans behind the war effort, the Committee of Public Information under George Creel was set up. Wilson had feared war might damage freedom in the country. Now his fears would come true. The Creel Committee made movies showing the barbarity of the "Huns" as the Germans were called. Pamphlets were printed saying that the German people had always been evil. Hatred against all that was German was stirred up. The German language was no longer taught in the schools. German books were taken from libraries. Dachshunds, a German breed of dog, were now called liberty pups, and the German cabbage dish known as sauerkraut was now liberty cabbage. But the worst was yet to come.

Wilson himself approved the Espionage Act of 1917. This law provided a prison term of twenty years for anyone who criticized the military draft or spoke in a disloyal way. Later, the Sedition Act of 1918 punished people for anything they did that might harm the war effort. Under these laws hundreds of people were arrested and jailed. For example, Eugene V. Debs, a socialist politician, said the United States was not democratic. For spreading this opinion, he was sentenced to ten years in prison.

Ordinary Americans were spied on by the government. Mail was opened and read, and telephones were bugged so the government could make sure people were not speaking in a disloyal way. Wilson said this surveillance was "dangerous" to freedom, but he did nothing to stop it.[9] Even after the war ended, Wilson refused to pardon Eugene Debs. Wilson said he could never again look a soldier in the eye if he pardoned Debs and others who might have weakened the war effort.[10]

Wartime conditions led to two other dramatic changes in American life. For decades in the United States the temperance movement had fought to ban liquor. During World War I patriotism became blended with the temperance movement because so many beer brewers were German. Also, antiliquor forces argued that precious resources should not be wasted on making liquor during war. Wilson opposed banning liquor, but the Eighteenth Amendment passed Congress in December 1917. This amendment prohibited the making and selling of liquor.

Fighting World War I cost a lot of money. The highest taxes in United States history were passed. The government also took over the production of everything from food to machines. Wilson wanted to make sure the soldiers had all they needed to fight the war. Everything else took second place. Once, when Wilson heard that some soldiers did not have decent shelter or clothing, he got fighting mad. One senator said, "His jaw was set. His eyes shot fire."[11] On that occasion, Wilson took over the production lines himself to get the needed materials to the military.

World War I had serious economic consequences for the United States and the world. The Allies borrowed

SOURCE DOCUMENT

World War I fundraising posters and buttons

millions from the United States. More money was printed and this led to serious inflation after the war. Some businesses had to be shut down when their workers were drafted. The shift to war materials disrupted normal economic life. This disruption led in part to the Great Depression of the 1930s.

The first important American battle was fought in June 1918, at Château-Thierry, a village about fifty miles from Paris. The Germans were attacking in a small forest nearby called Belleau Wood. Thousands of United States Marines rushed into the woods to help the French. The Marines won, but over five thousand were killed or wounded.

In September 1918, the Americans joined with the French to attack St. Mihiel Salient, a German stronghold on the Meuse River, south of Verdun. After two days of fighting, there were seven thousand Americans who had been killed or wounded.

From September 1918 to November 1918, Americans took part in the biggest, bloodiest campaign of the war—the Meuse-Argonne offensive. One hundred twenty thousand Americans were killed or wounded. But the end of the war was in sight. In the fall of 1918, the Allies were winning all over. The German army was falling apart and the German people were starving because of the blockade set up by the Allies. There were food riots in Germany as people searched garbage pails for scraps to stay alive. On November 11, 1918, the Germans agreed to stop fighting. The Central Powers

On September 26, 1918, American fighting men are shown occupying a German trench in the Argonne region of France during a break in the battle.

and the Allies met in a railroad car in a French forest to sign the agreement that would end the war. World War I was over at last.

World War I had taken the lives of 10 million soldiers and other military. More died in this war than in all wars in the preceding one hundred years. About 21 million soldiers were wounded. Many were blinded or had lost limbs. Thousands of young men would spend the rest of their lives as invalids. Nobody knows how many civilians died of disease, starvation, and other war-related causes. Property damage was about $337 billion. World War I had cost about $10 million an hour during 1918. The battles had wrecked tens of thousands of homes and businesses. Farms and villages were destroyed. Factories were burned down. Bridges

President Wilson marches in the Liberty Day parade in New York City, October 1918. Dr. Cary Grayson (third from right) devoted all his time to making sure the president remained healthy.

and railroad tracks were blown up. Much of Europe looked like a burned-out ghost town.

The Allies had won the war. They blamed Germany and the other Central Powers for causing all the ruin and misery. When the war ended, the winners, especially Britain and France, plotted revenge. Germany would be made to pay for all the suffering the Allies had endured. The Allies wanted Germany to be severely punished. They wanted Germany to be so completely crushed that it could never wage war again.

Long before World War I ended, Woodrow Wilson had a much different plan in mind. He dreamed of all nations, both the Allies and Central Powers, coming together. There would be justice for all. Everybody would sit down together and plan for a better world. Wilson knew that revenge breeds revenge. The history of humanity is of war, followed by revenge, followed by new wars. Wilson wanted to end this terrible cycle of violence. Wilson had led his nation to victory in war—now he wanted to lead the world to peace. Wilson wanted World War I to be "the war to end all wars."[12]

Wilson's plan was called the Fourteen Points. These were the basic ideas in his plan: All nations had the right to rule themselves. This included colonial peoples (nations like India and Africa, which were ruled by European powers like Britain and France). There would be freedom of the seas—ships of all nations could travel without harm, and countries could trade freely with one another. Armaments, like tanks and bombs, would be reduced. The most important idea of all was the formation of a League of Nations.

All nations would belong to the League of Nations. If a fight started between two nations, they would not turn to war to settle it. They would take it to the court of the League of Nations. All conflicts would be settled peacefully. This was the dream that Wilson hoped to sell to America and the world.

8

THE LEAGUE OF NATIONS

A peace conference was held in Paris in January 1919. There the Allies would decide on the terms of peace. They would draw up a peace treaty to be signed by the losers—the Central Powers. Woodrow Wilson decided to attend the peace conference personally. He could have sent his secretary of state, but this was just too important to him. He wanted the League of Nations to be part of the Treaty of Paris.

Wilson's ship, the *George Washington*, left New York on December 4, 1918. Wilson arrived in Brest, France, and was greeted as a great hero. Thousands of people came to welcome him. Signs carried by the people read, "Hail the champion of the rights of man," "Honor to the founder of the society of nations," and other such words of praise.[1]

December 1918—Wilson stands on the deck of the ship George Washington *en route from America to France, where he was heralded as a hero for helping end World War I.*

In Paris, thousands more turned out to hail Wilson. Bouquets of violets almost buried the carriage carrying Mr. and Mrs. Wilson.[2] When Wilson arrived in Rome, the streets had been sprinkled with gold dust. In Milan, Italy, the crowds were almost hysterical when they saw Wilson. They shouted greetings like "Wilson, savior of humanity," and "The Moses from across the Atlantic."[3] Italian families placed candles next to photographs of Wilson. All over Europe "Saint Woodrow" was

President Wilson and French President Raymond Poincaré greeting cheering crowds in Paris, France, on December 14, 1918.

honored.[4] Word had reached these war-weary people that here was a man about to build a new world forever at peace. Raymond Fosdick, Wilson's former student, wrote sympathetically, "Poor Wilson! A man with his responsibility was to be pitied."[5]

Although the Europeans were cheering him, Wilson knew he had determined political enemies at home. Republicans in the Senate had not wanted Wilson to lead the American delegation to Paris. They wanted someone else to go. The mood in the Senate toward Wilson was "sullen and quiet."[6]

Wilson was physically exhausted, but he was determined to do a good job at Paris. He believed the world would never forgive him if he failed to fight for a just and lasting peace.[7]

Britain's delegation was led by David Lloyd George. Lloyd George wanted Germany to pay for all the war damages to Britain. He had been elected Prime Minister of Great Britain on the slogan "make Germany pay."[8] Italy's Vittorio Orlando wanted land for his country. He wanted part of the Austria-Hungary empire to be given to Italy. Georges Clemenceau, Premier of France, was nicknamed the "tiger of France." He was a tough-minded man who wanted Germany crushed and driven into poverty so the Germans could never threaten France again.[9]

Long before Wilson got to the peace conference, the Europeans had made secret treaties with each other. The terms of these secret deals were opposed to

President Wilson, in 1918, spends Christmas Day in France with AEF troops. The next year he would return to witness the drafting of the Treaty of Versailles.

Wilson's Fourteen Points. European leaders plotted to block Wilson's agenda.[10]

Wilson studied furiously in Paris so he would be prepared for the conference issues. There was disagreement on returning land taken during the war and on granting self-government to colonial peoples. For the Europeans a big issue was reparations—making Germany pay huge sums to repair the damage of World War I. The trouble with this plan was that Germany was badly damaged by the war, too, and could not afford to pay damages.

Wilson sits with leaders of Europe who were opposed to his Fourteen Points. Seated left to right at the Hôtel de Crillon, Paris, France, December 1918: Premier Orlando of Italy, Premier Lloyd George of England, Premier Clemenceau of France, and President Wilson

The Treaty of Versailles was written in April 1919. In June Germany accepted the terms. It had no choice because it had lost the war. Wilson had not wanted Germany to be forced to pay high reparations, but he gave in to this point as a trade-off to get his League of Nations. An observer at the Paris peace conference, John Maynard Keynes wrote that the reparations would skin Germany alive. Keynes called the arrangement "one of the most outrageous acts of a cruel victor in civilized history." He predicted that Germany would be reduced to miserable poverty. He predicted that, as a result, another, more terrible war would come about in the future.[11] This was exactly what happened when, about twenty years later, World War II broke out.

Back in the United States, the Nineteenth Amendment passed Congress in June 1919. President Wilson favored giving American women the same right to vote that men had. After decades of struggle, the women's suffrage movement saw victory. The sacrifices American women made during World War I, at home and on the battlefields where thousands served as nurses and in communications, helped turn the tide.

On July 8, 1919, Wilson returned to New York. Ten thousand cheering people greeted him. But trouble came quickly. Many Americans did not like the treaty Wilson brought home. German Americans said it was unfair to Germany. Others complained that the League of Nations would get the United States mixed up in more European squabbles. These people were called isolationists. They wanted the United States to stay out of foreign affairs.

Wilson highlighted the good points of the Treaty of Versailles. New countries like Czechoslovakia and Yugoslavia had been created, giving self-government to people once hidden in old empires. European boundaries were changed to restore the independence of Poland. But for Wilson and the Senate, the heart of the treaty was the League of Nations and American membership in the League. Wilson saw these provisions as the path to world peace.

In July, Wilson went to the Senate to ask them to

Although many Americans didn't like the Treaty of Versailles, it did mark the official ending of the war. Here, months before, Wilson and General Pershing say good-bye to American troops after review on December 25, 1918.

vote for the treaty. Wilson was very weak from the months of hard work in Paris. He read his speech very slowly. Sometimes he stumbled over words. Wilson may have suffered another small stroke in Paris.

Wilson told the senators that the United States could not turn back from its role as leader of the world. "America shall in truth show the way. The light streams upon the path ahead and nowhere else,"[12] Wilson said. "Dare we reject it and break the heart of the world?"[13]

After the war, the Treaty of Versailles needed to be approved by Congress. Above, at a 1918 Christmas dinner in France, are some of the people who helped end the war. Left to right: Cary T. Grayson, Rear Admiral USN; Major General McAndrew, Chief of Staff AEF; Mrs. Wilson; General Pershing; and Wilson

When Wilson finished speaking, visitors in the Senate chamber applauded along with the Democrats. But Republican senators were quiet. The Republican leader was Massachusetts Senator Henry Cabot Lodge. He was chairman of the powerful Senate Foreign Relations Committee. The treaty had to get through that committee to pass.

Lodge disliked Wilson intensely.[14] Lodge wanted to make big changes in the treaty before he would vote for it. Other Republicans—called "irreconcilables"—were against the League, even more strongly. They would never vote for it.

Senator Lodge especially disliked Article 10 of the League of Nations. This article pledged that if any nation were threatened, all the other nations would come to its aid. Lodge did not want the United States promising to defend all those other countries. Lodge's position was that, "only Congress could authorize such intervention."[15]

Wilson felt that Article 10 was the heart of the League of Nations. He believed that if all nations promised to help each other against attack, no nation would be foolish enough to start a new war and take on the world. But Wilson could not bring the Senate around to his way of thinking. So he decided to take his case directly to the American people. If the people were on his side, surely the Senate would have to support the treaty and the League of Nations.

In September 1919, Wilson began the train trip he

hoped would win over the hearts of the American people. He was drawing great, cheering crowds when he became seriously ill and was forced to cut his tour short. The train rushed back to Washington.

When Wilson arrived in Washington, he seemed a little better. He was able to walk from the train to his automobile. Over the next two days he improved even more. Then, he got one of his bad headaches again. On October 1, Wilson went to his room early to sleep. After a little while, Edith Wilson went to check on him. She

The Big Four in Paris in 1919; from left to right: Lloyd George, Orlando, Clemenceau, and Wilson. Wilson hoped these world leaders, as well as the American public, would endorse the League of Nations.

found Wilson sitting on the side of the bed trying to drink water. His left hand hung limp. He could not bring the water glass to his lips. In another few minutes, Wilson sank to the floor, unconscious. Edith Wilson put a pillow under his head and covered him with a blanket.

Dr. Grayson and three other doctors rushed to the president's side. They found that he had suffered a major stroke. The entire left side of his body was left paralyzed.

9

A SICKLY PRESIDENT

There was a clot in the artery of Wilson's brain. For the next two and one half weeks Wilson was between life and death. But the American people did not know about the president's state. Edith Wilson did not want anybody to know how sick her husband was. She did not even tell Wilson himself that he had suffered a stroke.[1] Dr. Grayson told the American people that Wilson was very ill, that he was experiencing a nervous breakdown and indigestion. Most people concluded that the president had been working too hard and was now having a much-needed rest.

Nobody was permitted to see Wilson except the doctors; his secretary, Joseph Tumulty; his daughters; and of course, Mrs. Wilson. A careful cocoon of secrecy was spun around the president. Secretary of State Lansing wanted Vice-President Thomas Marshall to take over the presidency during Wilson's illness. Edith Wilson refused. "I am not thinking of the country now," she said, "I am thinking of my husband."[2] It would be nearly forty years before this problem of a sick president was dealt with by law. The Twenty-fifth Amendment, ratified in 1967, allowed a president to be declared too ill to do his duties. In such a situation the vice-president then becomes acting president.

Wilson was paralyzed, and he also had kidney trouble. He was too weak to understand the issues of the presidency. He remained between life and death from October 2, 1919, to late January 1920.

Mrs. Wilson and Dr. Grayson acted as an informal government. When documents required the president's signature, they would thrust them into Wilson's shaky hands and guide him to scrawl his name. Mrs. Wilson was a steward and she never claimed to have made decisions on behalf of the president.[3] Yet, quite clearly, she was deciding which issues needed attention and which might be ignored. So, in effect, she acted for her husband, the president.

Members of the Wilson administration argued about what to do. Secretary of State Lansing wanted Dr. Grayson to declare Wilson too ill to be president. But Joseph Tumulty, Wilson's secretary, was fiercely loyal. He insisted that Wilson had always been too kind to him and now he would refuse to allow him to be taken from the White House.[4]

Not even Vice-President Marshall knew how sick Wilson was. Marshall asked for more information. He feared that if he were suddenly called on to be president he would not even know what was going on.[5]

Rumors ran wild in Washington. Some hinted that Wilson had lost his mind. Europeans worried that the Treaty of Versailles was doomed if Wilson did not get well. *The London Daily Chronicle*, which supported the League of Nations, called Wilson the "peoples' hope."[6]

During this time the Senate debated the Treaty of Versailles and membership in the League of Nations. In his moments of clear thinking, Wilson asked about it. He was told the battle was going well. Edith Wilson tried hard to keep any bad news from him. But it was a difficult task. She complained about how hard it was to protect him while the nation expected him to be their leader.[7]

When Vice-President Marshall finally learned how sick Wilson was, he put his face into his hands and then stared into space. Suspicious senators studied Wilson's recent signatures with microscopes. They tried to prove that someone else was forging Wilson's name, but they could not. Edith Wilson waited for her husband to have a good day, or a few good hours, to get the president's signature down on documents.

On October 17, Wilson was again near death, suffering a kidney blockage. But once again he survived. By December a bitter joke was going around the Senate. Every time a document bearing Wilson's signature arrived, senators laughed and said, "Here is something else from

Tumulty."[8] Secretary of State Lansing felt sure that others were acting as well as thinking for the president. He feared the truth would get out, causing a big scandal.[9]

By December 6, Wilson felt well enough to meet with two senators. Wilson was stretched out on his bed, his left arm hidden beneath a blanket. A single light was carefully placed to keep him in shadow. Wilson managed to speak a little.[10] As sick as he was, Wilson sensed how hostile many senators were toward him, and he tried valiantly to appear better than he was.

In November 1919, the Senate had defeated the Treaty of Versailles and United States membership in the League of Nations. Four months later, in March 1920, they voted again. Wilson was urged to accept some amendments to the treaty. Then maybe it would have passed. But Wilson refused to do this. Some say his poor health harmed his judgment. Others said he was a stubborn man all his life who would not budge. When Wilson was told to compromise he said, "Let Lodge compromise!"[11] And then he added, "better a thousand times to go down fighting than to dip your colors to dishonorable compromise."[12]

On March 19, 1920, the treaty was sent back to Wilson with the message that it had been killed. This meant the United States would not benefit from his creation of the League of Nations. A sad Woodrow Wilson said, "I feel like going to bed and staying there."[13] Wilson asked Dr. Grayson to read to him from the Bible, which he did. Then Wilson said, "Doctor, if I were not a

Christian I think I should go mad, but my faith in God holds me to the belief that He is in some way working out His own plans."[14]

The 1920 presidential election loomed. Wilson had considered running for a third term, but with his health so bad that was now impossible. Wilson had all he could do to learn to walk again. When he was supported by

SOURCE DOCUMENT

This cartoon illustrates the rejection by the Senate of U.S. membership in the League of Nations. Senator William Borah (R Idaho), Senator Henry Cabot Lodge (R Massachusetts), and Senator Hiram Johnson (R California) all led the opposition to Wilson's fight for the League.

someone's arm, he could drag his left leg along. He took one slow, painful step at a time. He forced himself over and over to climb stairs. But as much as he tried, he could never again rise from a chair without help.

Those who visited the White House always found Wilson seated, wrapped in a blanket. He wore a golf cap pulled down low on his face. He was now completely blind in one eye. His face showed the effects of his serious illness. One visitor said Wilson's mouth hung open all the time, making him appear senile.[15] Another visitor noted how sick he looked, and how thin he was, with a drooping jaw and "staring, almost unseeing eyes."[16]

However, Wilson's mind was clear during this time. He wrote about his daily routine. He struggled from one part of the house to the other. He went through his daily work, but he was afraid nothing he did mattered anymore.[17] Wilson was told by Dr. Grayson that he was slowly getting better, but in fact Wilson did not see much improvement.

The Democratic nominee for president in 1920 was Ohio Governor James A. Cox. Cox went to the White House to pay his respects to Wilson. He promised Wilson that he would try very hard to get the Senate to change its mind on the League of Nations. He promised to fight for it as hard as Wilson had fought.[18]

Once more, Wilson's hopes rose. If Cox became president, perhaps the League of Nations might still become a powerful force for world peace. Perhaps the United States would join. It all depended on the election of 1920.

10

A MAN OF PEACE

T he Republicans in 1920 chose Ohio Senator
Warren G. Harding for their candidate. Harding
opposed the League of Nations. During the
campaign Cox was true to his promise. He supported
American membership in the League of Nations. Wilson
was sure Cox would win. "The American people will not
turn Cox down and elect Harding," he said. "A great
moral issue is involved. The people can and will see it."[1]

But in November Harding won by a landslide. He
got 16 million votes. Cox got 9 million. The Republicans
said the election was a vote on the League of Nations.
"So far as the United States is concerned," a happy
Senator Henry Cabot Lodge said, "that League is
dead."[2] But Wilson clung to the hope that someday his
principles would win. "I have not lost faith in the

SOURCE DOCUMENT

2340 S STREET N

WOODROW WILSON

WASHINGTON D C

JUL 15 1921

BUREAU OF INDEXES AND ARCHIVES
RECEIVED
JUN ... 1921
DEPARTMENT OF STATE

15th July 1921

My dear Mr. Secretary:

When the Treaty of Versailles failed of ratification by the Senate the copy of the Treaty accompanying this note was returned to me personally with the official notification from the Senate that votes sufficient for the ratification could not be obtained.

This was at the time I was very ill, and the copy was put in my private fireproof files for safekeeping, and when my effects were transferred from The White House to my presence residence this copy of the Treaty was of course transferred with other papers under the conditions of safety with which it had at all times been surrounded.

I beg now that if it is convenient to you, you will permit me to deposit it with the Department of State. I am therefore sending the copy by my secretary along with this letter.

Cordially yours,

Woodrow Wilson

Honorable Charles E. Hughes,
Secretary of State,
Washington, D. C.

FILED
JUN 24 1922

P.S. I know that your judgment will justify me in asking the favor of having a formal receipt sent me for this copy.

W. W.

In 1921, Wilson sent a copy of the Treaty of Versailles, along with this letter, to Charles Evans Hughes, his former opponent, who was now secretary of state under Warren G. Harding.

American people," he said. "They have merely been temporarily deceived. They will realize their error in a little while."[3]

As Wilson finished out the last weeks of his presidency, his health changed from day to day. Sometimes he was calm and bright but other times he had angry spells. He suffered spells of weeping.[4] "It is an uphill work and the hill is very steep," Wilson said of his struggle to regain his health.[5]

In early December of 1920, Wilson was awarded the Nobel Peace Prize for 1919. He was honored for his role in creating the League of Nations, although the United States never became a member.

On March 4, 1921, Harding was inaugurated. Wilson had a hard time getting into his coat and gray trousers. But he wanted to be there. He rode in an open car toward the inauguration ceremony. He was a "slumped and frail figure."[6] He was not able to walk to the reviewing stand. He slipped away quickly and returned to the White House.

The Wilsons left the White House quietly. They moved to a house on S Street in Washington. The Wilsons had a small income from royalties on his books. But they did not have enough money to live well. Back then, presidents did not receive pensions. A group of friends got together and raised some money. They gave Wilson an annuity—an income of ten thousand dollars a year for life. Wilson said of the gesture, "my heart is overflowing. I am deeply proud that such men should think me worthy of such benefits."[7]

During Wilson's retirement, Edith Wilson spent many hours reading to her husband. The Wilsons took many rides in the Pierce-Arrow he had used at the White House. The Wilsons bought the car from the United States government. Sometimes the Wilsons went to baseball games. They parked on the outfield so Wilson could watch the game in privacy. He was so frail he did not want to mix with the crowds, and it was hard for him to walk very far. Wilson lived the life of an

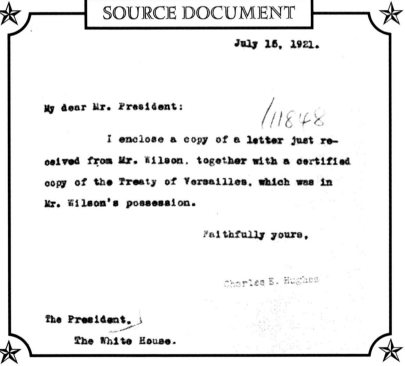

Hughes' letter, relaying Wilson's copy of the Treaty of Versailles to President Harding.

invalid. There were few visitors. Wilson's meals were often taken in bed.

On Armistice Day, November 11, 1921, President Harding invited Wilson to take part in the ceremonies. The burial of the unknown soldier from World War I was to take place. All of the nations that fought in World War I had a memorial to soldiers killed during the war. America's Unknown Soldier was buried at Arlington National Cemetery in Arlington, Virginia. He was brought home from France and then placed in a tomb. The inscription on the grave reads, "Here rests in honored glory an American soldier known but to God."

The Wilsons arrived in a carriage. A murmur went up from the crowd. When the people saw Wilson, applause broke out. After the ceremony, as Wilson returned home to S Street, he was surprised to find twenty thousand cheering people.[8] Leaning on his cane, Wilson tried to speak to the people. "I can only say God bless you," he said.[9] As the crowd went on cheering, Wilson steadied himself by grasping Edith Wilson's hand. Tears rolled down Wilson's cheeks. A reporter wrote, "the grief of the trembling man" touched the crowd and they wept openly.[10]

Wilson joined a law firm as a partner, but he could never practice law. He wanted to return to his writing career. He hoped to write a book, but he did not have the strength. He could only manage to write a brief article—"The Road Away from Revolution." It was published in the *Atlantic Monthly*. In this article he pleaded for a social order based on "sympathy and helpfulness."[11] Wilson urged people to ignore their own self-interest and worry about the happiness of others. He asked that the "spirit of Christ" fill the world.[12]

In November 1923, Wilson made a brief speech. He said that his principles would triumph someday. "That we shall prevail is as sure as that God reigns," he said.[13] He felt that someday there would be a world organization working for peace. He was right.

In fact, about twenty-five years after the Senate rejected United States membership in the League of Nations, the United Nations was created. The United States was a founding member. The United Nations was similar in structure to the League of Nations. It placed even stronger obligations on members to oppose aggression. But the difference was that the Republicans and the Democrats were working together in the Senate and isolationism was not a strong force anymore.

Wilson's health slowly improved until late in 1923. In December 1923, Wilson celebrated his sixty-seventh birthday. One month later he grew very ill again. News spread that Wilson was dying. A large crowd gathered outside the Wilson home on S Street. Many of the people carried candles. Wilson grew weaker and weaker. Finally he said to Dr. Grayson, "the machinery is broke. I am ready."[14]

At 11:15 on Sunday morning, February 3, 1924, Woodrow Wilson died. The crowds waiting outside knelt in the street as church bells tolled. Flags all over the country dropped to half mast.

Woodrow Wilson was buried in a crypt in Washington Cathedral on Mount St. Alban, the highest point in the city. The funeral was held on February 6. There was no lying in state, nor were there any military displays. Edith Wilson made these decisions. Senator Henry Cabot Lodge was scheduled to lead a delegation from Congress to the funeral. Edith Wilson told him he would be unwelcome, so he did not come.[15] President Calvin Coolidge, who succeeded Warren Harding in

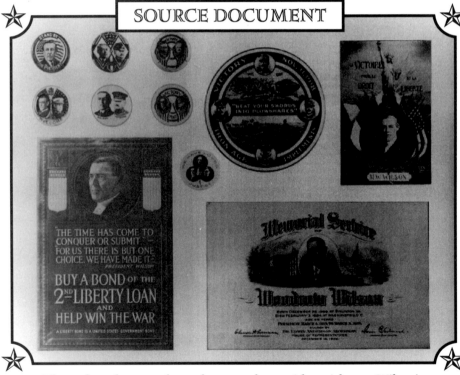

Liberty loan banners from the war, along with a ticket to Wilson's funeral

office, led the government delegation. A simple stone was placed over Wilson's grave. It read, "Woodrow Wilson, born December 28 1856 Died February 3 1924."

Right after Wilson died he was evaluated by historians. Some blamed him for getting the United States mixed up in World War I. Some blamed him for failing to fulfill his dream of peace. Historian Frederick Jackson Turner said, "Fate has dealt harshly with him but Time, the great restorer, and, let us believe history, will do him justice."[16]

Wilson was forced to spend most of his time dealing with foreign policy. But he preferred to deal with domestic issues, and he was a successful president at home. He reorganized the United States money system with the Federal Reserve Act. He promoted free trade. He made life better for working people.

Wilson has been called a "great leader" because he understood the dreams of plain people and expressed them.[17] Wilson was credited as a prophet too. Wilson warned that if the League of Nations failed, another more terrible war would break out, and it did.[18] About twenty years after the end of World War I, World War II broke out. Wilson dared to dream of stopping war forever. But Wilson often acted as if he were right and his opponents were totally wrong. This attitude annoyed many people. Wilson's biggest fault may have been his stubborn pride.[19]

Economist John Maynard Keynes who was at the Paris Peace Conference was very hard on Wilson. He said Wilson was less intelligent than the British and French leaders. He blamed Wilson for digging in his toes and refusing to compromise.[20]

According to another historian, Wilson was carried away by the cheering crowds who greeted him in Europe after World War I. He found it hard to believe that the world was not behind him. He could not understand the British and the French leaders not following his lead. Then when he returned home, he could not believe the Senate refused to allow the United States to join the League of Nations. Because he was so sure he was right, he refused compromise. That destroyed his chances for having the United States participate in the League of Nations. "With his own sickly hands Wilson slew his own brain child."[21]

The most credible historical assessment of President Wilson praises him for his relentless pursuit of world peace. He was willing to sacrifice even himself for this noble goal. Also, forces opposing him both in Paris and Washington were powerful and often vicious. Yet he failed his own dream by refusing to compromise.[22]

Woodrow Wilson was a noble and idealistic man. All through his life he tried to do what was right. He acted that way as president of Princeton University and as president of the United States. Because his desire to build a peaceful world was his greatest dream, he was willing to risk his life in a harrowing train trip. Wilson must have known from his weariness and his headaches that he was pushing his body dangerously. His doctor warned him. He said he did not care. Wilson believed that if he made just one more speech he might win the fight for peace. He was, in the end, a casualty of World War I. He sent thousands of young men into battle during that war. He believed he owed them his last-ditch effort to end all future wars.

In a 1945 speech, President Harry Truman honored the United Nations. He said that Woodrow Wilson's dream had finally come true. From now on, there would be a world organization to prevent future world wars.[23] Jan Christiaan Smuts, a South-African statesman who supported Wilson, said "Americans of the future will yet proudly and gratefully rank him with Washington and Lincoln."[24]

Chronology

1856—Born in Staunton, Virginia.

1875—Entered Princeton University.

1879—Entered University of Virginia Law School.

1882—Passed the bar exam and became a lawyer.

1885—Married Ellen Axson.

1886—Received Ph.D. from Johns Hopkins University; First child, Margaret, born. Began teaching at Bryn Mawr College.

1887—Second daughter, Jessie, born.

1888—Began teaching at Wesleyan University.

1889—Third child, Eleanor, born.

1890—Hired to teach at Princeton University.

1902—Became president of Princeton College.

1911—Became governor of New Jersey.

1912—Elected president of the United States.

1913—Federal Reserve Act—most important domestic achievement of administration.

1914—Death of Ellen Axson Wilson; Beginning of World War I.

1915—Married Edith Bolling Galt.

1916—Elected to second term as president.

1917—Declaration of war against Germany and Central Powers.

1919—Attended peace conference in Paris—helped draw up Treaty of Versailles. Founded League of Nations.

1920—Awarded Nobel Peace Prize.

1924—Died in Washington, D.C.

Chapter Notes

Chapter 1

1. Tom Shachtman, *Edith & Woodrow* (New York: G.P. Putnam's Sons, 1981), p. 173.
2. Cary T. Grayson, *Woodrow Wilson: An Intimate Memoir* (New York: Holt, Rinehart & Winston, 1960), p. 94.
3. Arthur S. Link, *Woodrow Wilson* (Chicago: Quadrangle Paperbacks, 1972), p. 164.
4. Kendrick A. Clements, *The Presidency of Woodrow Wilson* (Lawrence: University Press of Kansas, 1992), p. 195.
5. Link, p. 165.
6. Shachtman, p. 197.
7. August Heckscher, *Woodrow Wilson* (New York: Macmillan, 1991), p. 603.
8. Ibid., p. 604.
9. Thomas J. Knock, *To End All Wars* (Oxford: Oxford University Press, 1992), p. 263.
10. Shachtman, p. 203.
11. Ibid.
12. Ibid., p. 196.
13. Heckscher, p. 609.
14. Ibid.
15. Ibid., p. 610.
16. Clements, p. 197.
17. Ibid.
18. Ibid.
19. Shachtman, p. 205.
20. Ibid.

Chapter 2

1. August Heckscher, *Woodrow Wilson* (New York: Macmillan, 1991), p. 10.
2. Ray Stannard Baker, *Woodrow Wilson: Life and Letters* (Garden City: Doubleday, Page & Co., 1927), Vol. I. p. 28.

3. Arthur S. Link, *Woodrow Wilson* (Chicago: Quadrangle Paperbacks, 1972), p. 17.

4. Baker, p. 32.

5. Ibid., p. 33.

6. Ibid., p. 35.

7. Kendrick A. Clements, *The Presidency of Woodrow Wilson* (Lawrence: University Press of Kansas, 1992), p. 2.

8. Baker, p. 36.

9. Heckscher, p. 13.

10. Ibid., p. 23.

11. Baker, p. 59.

12. Heckscher, p. 26.

13. Ibid., p. 36.

14. Link, p. 19.

15. Baker, p. 36.

16. Heckscher, p. 46.

17. Ibid., p. 47.

18. John Milton Cooper, Jr., *The Warrior and the Priest: Woodrow Wilson and Theodore Roosevelt* (Cambridge, Mass.: Harvard University Press, 1983), p. 45.

Chapter 3

1. August Heckscher, *Woodrow Wilson* (New York: Macmillan, 1991), p. 60.

2. Ibid., p. 63.

3. Ibid.

4. Tom Shachtman, *Edith & Woodrow* (New York: G.P. Putnam's Sons, 1981), p. 23.

5. Heckscher, p. 75.

6. Woodrow Wilson, *Congressional Government* (New York: Meridian, 1959), p. 185.

7. Ibid., p. 133.

8. Arthur S. Link, *Woodrow Wilson* (Chicago: Quadrangle Paperbacks, 1972), p. 23.

9. Heckscher, p. 106.

10. Ibid., p. 107.

11. Ibid., p. 108.

12. Link, p. 25.

13. Woodrow Wilson, *A History of the American People* (New York: Harper and Brothers Publishers, 1901), Vol. I, p. 345.

14. Link, p. 31.

15. Ibid., p. 33.

16. Ibid.

17. Heckscher, p. 184.

Chapter 4

1. Ray Stannard Baker, *Woodrow Wilson: Life and Letters* (New York: Harper & Row, 1931), Vol. III, p. 23.

2. Arthur S. Link, *Woodrow Wilson* (Chicago: Quadrangle Paperbacks, 1972), p. 43.

3. August Heckscher, *Woodrow Wilson* (New York: Macmillan, 1991), p. 227.

4. Ibid., p. 226.

5. Ibid., p. 233.

6. Ibid., p. 243.

7. Ibid., p. 235.

8. Woodrow Wilson, *Constitutional Government in the United States* (New York: Columbia University Press, 1908), p. 141.

9. George E. Mowry, *Theodore Roosevelt and the Progressive Movement* (Madison: University of Wisconsin Press, 1946), p. 256.

10. Ibid., p. 265.

11. Ibid., p. 277.

12. Tom Shachtman, *Edith & Woodrow* (New York: G.P. Putnam's Sons, 1981), p. 16.

13. Ibid., p. 15.

14. Heckscher, p. 274.

Chapter 5

1. Ray Stannard Baker and W.E. Dodd, eds., *The Public Papers of Woodrow Wilson* (New York: Harper & Row, 1925), Vol. I, p. 32.

2. Arthur S. Link, *Woodrow Wilson* (Chicago: Quadrangle Paperbacks, 1972), p. 74.

3. August Heckscher, *Woodrow Wilson* (New York: Macmillan, 1991), p. 281.

4. Heckscher, p. 322.

5. Heckscher, p. 323.

6. Tom Shachtman, *Edith & Woodrow* (New York: G.P. Putnam's Sons, 1981), p. 17.

7. Heckscher, p. 333.

8. Shachtman, p. 39.

9. Shachtman, p. 39.

10. Ibid., p. 52.

11. Ibid., p. 59.

12. Ibid., p. 54.

13. Ibid.

14. Lesley Byrd Simpson, *Many Mexicos* (Berkeley: University of California Press, 1964), p. 270.

15. Heckscher, p.299.

16. Ibid.

17. Link, p. 87.

18. Walter Mills, "Road to War," *Historians History of the United States* (New York: G.P. Putnam's Sons, 1966), Vol. II, p. 1134.

Chapter 6

1. Ray Stannard Baker and W. E. Dodd, eds., *The Public Papers of Woodrow Wilson: The New Democracy* (New York: Harper & Row, 1926), p. 282.

2. August Heckscher, *Woodrow Wilson* (New York: Macmillan, 1991), p. 347.

3. Tom Shachtman, *Edith & Woodrow* (New York: G.P. Putnam's Sons, 1981), p. 78.

4. Arthur S. Link, *Woodrow Wilson* (Chicago: Quadrangle Paperbacks, 1972), p. 95.

5. Ibid.

6. George E. Mowry, *Theodore Roosevelt and the Progressive Movement* (Madison: University of Wisconsin Press, 1946), p. 312.

7. Ibid., p. 315.

8. Heckscher, p. 356.

9. Julius W. Pratt, *A History of United States Foreign Policy.* (Englewood Cliffs, N.J.: Prentice-Hall, 1965), p. 272.

10. Kendrick A. Clements, *The Presidency of Woodrow Wilson* (Lawrence: University Press of Kansas, 1992), p. 52.

11. Albert Bushnell, ed., *Selected Addresses and Public Papers of Woodrow Wilson* (New York: Boni and Liveright, Inc., 1918), p. 118.

Chapter 7

1. William A. DeGregorio, *The Complete Book of U.S. Presidents* (New York: Dember Books, 1984), p. 424.

2. Tom Shachtman, *Edith & Woodrow* (New York: G.P. Putnam's Sons, 1981), p. 145.

3. Ibid., p. 147.

4. Ibid.

5. Ray Stannard Baker and W. E. Dodd, eds., *War and Peace: Presidential Messages, Addresses and Public Papers of Woodrow Wilson* (New York: Harper and Brothers, 1927), p. 158.

6. Walter Mills, "Road to War," *Historians History of the United States* (New York: G.P. Putnam's Sons, 1966), Vol. II, p. 1155.

7. Ibid., p. 1156.

8. Arthur S. Link, *Woodrow Wilson* (Chicago: Quadrangle Paperbacks, 1972), p. 117.

9. Kendrick A. Clements, *The Presidency of Woodrow Wilson* (Lawrence: University Press of Kansas, 1992), p. 155.

10. Link, p. 118.

11. Ibid., p. 123.

12. David Lloyd George, quoted on "World War I," PBS, March 28, 1976.

Chapter 8

1. Thomas J. Knock, *To End All Wars* (Oxford: Oxford University Press, 1992), p. 194.

2. Ibid., p. 195.

3. Ibid.

4. Ibid., p. 197.

5. August Heckscher, *Woodrow Wilson* (New York: Macmillan, 1991), p. 500.

6. Ibid., p. 496.

7. Arthur S. Link, *Woodrow Wilson* (Chicago: Quadrangle Paperbacks, 1972), p. 141.

8. Samuel Eliot Morison, *The Oxford History of the American People* (Oxford: Oxford University Press, 1965), p. 876.

9. Ibid.

10. Link, p. 145.

11. John Maynard Keynes, "Economic Consequences of the Peace," *Words That Made American History* (Boston: Little Brown & Company, 1962), p. 274.

12. Congressional Record, 66th Congress, 1st Session, July 10, 1919, p. 2339.

13. Link, p. 160.

14. Knock, p. 265.

15. Congressional Record, 66th Congress, 1st Session, p. 8773.

Chapter 9

1. Kendrick A. Clements, *The Presidency of Woodrow Wilson* (Lawrence: University Press of Kansas, 1992), p. 197.

2. Ibid., p. 198.

3. Ibid., p. 199.

4. Tom Shachtman, *Edith & Woodrow* (New York: G.P. Putnam's Sons, 1981), p. 211.

5. Ibid., p. 212.

6. Ibid.

7. Ibid., p. 214.

8. August Heckscher, *Woodrow Wilson* (New York: Macmillan, 1991), p. 621.

9. Ibid.

10. Ibid., p. 622.

11. Samuel Eliot Morison, *The Oxford History of the American People* (Oxford: Oxford University Press, 1965), p. 885.

12. Ibid.

13. Arthur S. Link, *Woodrow Wilson* (Chicago: Quadrangle Paperbacks, 1972), p. 173.

14. Ibid., p. 174.

15. Heckscher, p. 628.

16. Ibid.

17. Ibid., p. 639.

18. Ibid., p. 636.

Chapter 10

1. Arthur S. Link, *Woodrow Wilson* (Chicago: Quadrangle Paperbacks, 1972), p. 178.

2. Thomas J. Knock, *To End All Wars* (Oxford: Oxford University Press, 1992), p. 269.

3. Kendrick A. Clements, *The Presidency of Woodrow Wilson* (Lawrence: University Press of Kansas, 1992), p. 203.

4. Ibid.

5. August Heckscher, *Woodrow Wilson* (New York: Macmillan, 1991), p. 628.

6. Clements, p. 222.

7. Heckscher, p. 670.

8. Ibid., p. 658.

9. Ibid.

10. Ibid.

11. Link, p. 179.

12. Ibid.

13. Link, p. 180.

14. Tom Shachtman, *Edith & Woodrow* (New York: G.P. Putnam's Sons, 1981), p. 271.

15. Heckscher, p. 674.

16. Ibid., p. 644.

17. Samuel Eliot Morison, *The Oxford History of the American People* (Oxford: Oxford University Press, 1965), p. 886.

18. Ibid.

19. Ibid., p. 887.

20. John Maynard Keynes, "Economic Consequences of the Peace," *Words That Made American History* (Boston: Little Brown & Company, 1962), p. 268.

21. Thomas A. Bailey, "Woodrow Wilson and the Great Betrayal," *The Historians History of the United States* (New York: G.P. Putnam's Sons, 1966), Vol. II, p. 1187.

22. Arthur S. Link, *American Epoch* (New York: Alfred A. Knopf, 1963), p. 230.

23. Knock, p. 272.

24. Ibid., p. 276.

Further Reading

Baker, Ray Stannard. *Woodrow Wilson: Life and Letters.* Garden City: Doubleday, Page & Co., 1927.

Baker, Ray Stannard, and W. E. Dodd, eds. *The Public Papers of Woodrow Wilson.* Vol. I. New York: Harper & Row, 1925.

———. *The Public Papers of Woodrow Wilson: The New Democracy.* Vol. I. New York: Harper & Row, 1926.

———. *War and Peace: Presidential Messages, Addresses and Public Papers of Woodrow Wilson.* (1917–1924) Vol. I. New York: Harper & Brothers, 1927.

Bushnell, Albert, ed. *Selected Addresses and Public Papers of Woodrow Wilson.* New York: Boni and Liveright, Inc., 1918.

Clements, Kendrick A. *The Presidency of Woodrow Wilson.* Lawrence: University Press of Kansas, 1992.

Cooper, John Milton, Jr. *The Warrior and the Priest: Woodrow Wilson and Theodore Roosevelt.* Cambridge, Mass.: Harvard University Press, 1983.

Heckscher, August. *Woodrow Wilson.* New York: Scribner's, 1991.

Kent, Zachary. *World War I: "The War to End Wars."* Hillside, N.J.: Enslow Publishers, Inc., 1994.

Knock, Thomas J. *To End All Wars.* Oxford: Oxford University Press, 1992.

Link, Arthur S. *Woodrow Wilson.* Chicago: Quadrangle Paperbacks, 1972.

Shachtman, Tom. *Edith & Woodrow.* New York: G.P. Putnam's Sons, 1981.

Wilson, Woodrow. *Congressional Government.* New York: Meridian, 1959.

———. *Constitutional Government in the United States.* New York: Columbia University Press, 1908.

———. *A History of the American People.* Vols. I–V. New York: Harper & Brothers, 1901.

Internet Addresses

The Whitehouse

http://www.whitehouse.gov/history/presidents/ww28.html

Grolier Online

http://gi.grolier.com/presidents/ea/bios/28pwils.html

**The Woodrow Wilson International
Center for Scholars**

http://wwics.si.edu

Index